SEARCHING FOR ME

Sammantha Rials

Searching for Me
Copyright © 2019
by Sammantha Rials
All Rights Reserved

All rights reserved. No part of this book may be reproduced in any form or by any electronic or mechanical means including information storage and retrieval systems, without permission in writing from the author. The only exception is by a reviewer, who may quote short excerpts in a review.

* * *

Names, characters, places, and incidents in this poetry compilation are either are products of the author's imagination or are used fictitiously. Any resemblance to actual persons, living or dead, events, or locales is entirely coincidental.

This book is dedicated to those in search of who they are, what they want, and how they perceive their experiences. Human emotions are complicated and layered. I hope for all people to reach a point where they lose judgement and fear of their own thoughts and feelings.
This is something I continue to work on in myself, every day.
Love & Light

HERE AND THERE

I crave intensity and then wonder why I feel engulfed in everything all the time. I feel that I am an oxymoron and I open Pandora's Box before I even know that it's there.

I remember the first time I let someone love me. It's one of those things that happens before you give it permission to occur. I often look back and laugh, because I felt so much and so did they.

It's funny when you try to repaint pictures of moments in your head because the colors always change. I had this picture of him and I and it was blue for about two years and now it is almost yellow with hints of green. It always changes. I am always changing how I view what happened. Sometimes, I feel as though, he never happened. While some days, I wake up and my world is flooded by him.

* * *

MIRROR

Have you ever thought that maybe we are more afraid of embracing the light than we are the dark? We start to wonder whether or not we deserve this light and whether or not it will suddenly be taken away from us. So we run, sometimes as far as we possibly can from the good things around us. It isn't necessarily because we are self destructive, but rather because we fear that the best part of ourselves will only disappoint us. If you keep an idea in your mind of how wonderful something can be, it can be scary to actually find out if it will live up to your expectations.

Recently, I had a realization that I am more than anything that will bring me to dark places inside of myself. I am here and I am experiencing other people, as they experience me, and we all have our battles to sort out. Maybe I have gotten in the way of other people's demons, but that doesn't mean they are mine. I am only my own demons and what I choose to focus on.

I choose to acknowledge the good in the negative parts of my life, because I am only able to experience things from the depth that I allow myself to. I want to be able to understand true pain, so that I can feel true gratitude for what I have. I also choose to see the darkness in the light, and remind it to keep its voice down.

* * *

THE INFINITE

I got to this point where I had to ask myself why I was attracting such painful situations into my life. It was as if I was punishing myself. I want to have this beautiful life, and I am simultaneously asking for this, but waiting for people who do not deserve me to show their love to me.

I want to understand why people do what they do and I want to get to a point where the way they treat me does not have a negative effect on the way I feel about myself, but that is difficult to fully comprehend.

Personally, I have come to the conclusion that we subconsciously attract certain situations. I couldn't tell you why or how, but sometimes we create things without our own knowledge. For myself, I am deathly afraid of commitment, not because I don't know how to love others but because I don't know how to be outside of my ego and my expectations of reality.

I am heavily torn between different parts of myself.

AWARENESS

See, I would rather be disconnected. I wish this, but then I realize that I would not be the same person if I did not feel to these depths. I could go around and sleep with whoever I want and get that satisfaction and feeling of pleasure, but would I wake up confused with myself?

Who am I?

Am I okay?

Is what I am feeling okay?

I question myself a lot and I wonder why I am standing on a peak of self-awareness, with no knowledge of how to jump right in.

* * *

LET'S SAY NO

I like myself and what I have to offer to those around me. The issue is that I wonder if I could be better or if there is a "right way". I want to believe that there are not solid answers for questions that encompass emotion.

If there were, I hope I never find them.

※ ※ ※

WELL, YOU

I fabricated myself into you. It was a slow process but I wanted to become so important that you would never want to leave me. Yes, that is selfish and so toxic. I waited to become entangled in someone again. You just seemed to fit a mold that I had long awaited.

Maybe a part of me knew that this all would happen and I would feel such intensity, and such pain. I wish I had given myself away to someone who knew how to take care of my soul and give it back to me when I was ready.

I remember looking into your eyes and thinking that I could look into them for the rest of my life. I wanted that, I wanted that stability. In reality though, I wasn't even ready to settle down with certain parts of myself.

* * *

THE ENDING

I looked at him, and in an instant, I forgave him.

"Look, you didn't know. Nobody does. We are floundering around trying to figure all this shit out. We hide behind religion and other forms of practice, but we have no clue how all of this works.

There is no foolproof guidebook to love or to people or to relationships. It doesn't work like that. I know you didn't mean to hurt me and I am always going to love you.

No matter what we do or what we say, we are bound to certain people. I have accepted that I am bound to you. Now, you have to accept that. Then, we can both move on."

* * *

MY BAD

Forgive me for not allowing you to really love me.
I know you wanted to.
I am so sorry.
I was far too afraid to let you in.
You never would have let me in either,
But it doesn't matter.
Would you?
I still see you,
Everywhere.
It doesn't hurt anymore.
I want to ask you about yourself.
I want to know everything about you.
Would you tell me, if I asked?

※ ※ ※

LONG, LONG TIME AGO

I don't know if you realize, but I am waiting for the day that the thought of you doesn't cause any reaction in me.

I like to say that I am indifferent to everything that occurred with us, but that is far from the truth. It is more that I have accepted that there is no way I can get what I want from the situation. Sometimes I remember everything, and it makes my head hurt and my heart heavy. There was a day when you told me that it would physically kill you to be with someone else and I wonder if you meant that. God knows, I wished you did in that moment.

Now, I don't have any way of differentiating what you meant from what you didn't mean. The irony is that it doesn't necessarily matter anymore. Regardless of what you felt or what you said, nothing can change what you did. For years, I wished that it could. I was waiting for something to make sense and click for me. I was waiting to hear from you and to know that it was all real and that it wasn't just a game.

Whether it was a game or not, I am done playing. That is all I have to say to you.

* * *

MISUNDERSTOOD

I spent a good three years trying to understand myself and how I felt about and perceived love. I worked really hard on learning about acceptance and letting people close to me.

Then, you came along.

I'm not mad anymore, but you took all of my progress and smashed it into a brick wall. I mean, it was all still there but it was in pieces on the ground and my feet had been stabbed by the ruins. You had made me bleed for so long that I would have fully bled out for you and not even noticed.

Is that what love really is?

I do not think so. I think love is an ever present feeling of consistency. No matter how bad it gets, you want that person to be happy. Don't get me wrong, their happiness does not come first, yours does. The point, is that you think about the way they feel, and you do it without trying.

I couldn't tell you why I kept picking people who didn't validate my feelings. It taught me that I, myself, must ALWAYS validate myself. Feelings can't be wrong and somehow we got this twisted a long time ago.

EVERYTHING

I want to say something before everything goes away and we are no longer in the same position that we are in right now.

God gives us these bodies and these minds and then we get to choose who we want to share them with. I've made some really good choices, and then some bad ones.

You, my dear, are not even a decision. It is an autopilot reaction to share my soul with yours. I want to give you everything I have inside of me.

I love you, in the most intimate and fire-filled way. You make me feel more alive than anyone or anything ever has. I crave every piece of your mind, as well as every cell of your body.

If I were to pick you apart, I would probably find slivers of myself already inside of you. I am well aware that we have fully merged into one and I could not be happier.

* * *

Sammantha Rials

* * *

US VERSUS US

It was short, the time that we spent together. I remember wanting there to be so much more time, especially because it was so substantial compared to everything else I had experienced. We were two people that had so much to offer, and together, we found mutual understanding of how much it took to give and also to take.

Sometimes, I like to think that we were just too good together and that is why it didn't work. I'm not sure why the universe works the way it does or how any of this stuff is decided. You and I were good together though.

It was almost like the moment you finally see yourself clearly, all that you are and all that you are not. Falling in love with you, was like that. It was clarity that I can't even explain to this day.

We were happy in a way that served nobody but us. It wasn't toxic, however. We just burned out so fast and it had nothing to do with feelings. It had everything to do with timing and circumstance.

If I run into you again one day, I hope I am found anew once more. I wantyou to show me myself, in full picture. I can only hope that this time, you will see yourself as well.

SOON

The world is made up of moments and series of time. We experience things in different order. It is the first moment that often becomes the image engraved in your memory. The first moment that you feel something so intensely and you cannot even imagine the gravity of what the emotion means.

I felt you, all over me. In my skull, in my solar plexus, in my gut, in my pelvis. I wanted to become one with the best parts of you and then everything else. It was like I hadn't been with anyone in this way before. Your touch was mesmerizing and overwhelming. I wanted to feel that sensation for the rest of my life. The earth felt vast and unending when I was with you. Every possibility was present and awakened.

There was nothing you could have done to stop me from falling into you. I had already decided what I wanted. I don't think you could have even warned me. I wouldn't have listened.

It wasn't you, and it wasn't me. It was time.

But before we know it, we will have our time and it will not be cut short.

* * *

FABRICATION

They want to tell you that people who love you won't hurt you. That is not true and that is not valid. Sometimes, if you feel too much, then you manifest pain through the infliction of more pain. It doesn't make it right and it does not take away from what the other person is doing, but it explains so much.

I think we create these ideas surrounding how people should respond in situations and experiences of emotions. These ideas do not necessarily correlate with reality and it tends to skew our minds.

I want to imagine that everything we do is purely thought out with intention, but it isn't always. We sometimes act on impulse and screw up incredible things. Whether it be out of fear or the simple fact that we have no clue how lucky we are.

Regardless, we act on momentary thoughts and at times, we spend the rest of our lives wondering why we couldn't have hesitated for just a moment longer.

BLISS

I laid there, watching your eyes flicker. You were half asleep and waking to the sight of me. I remember thinking, I would give anything to be eternally the first thing you would see, each and every day.

* * *

THE CLOSENESS

People always told me that intimacy was something you couldn't explain. I understand that now. Most of the time, it depends on the person and the relationship you have cultivated with them. It depends on the two people in the situation and how their facets work together.

* * *

NEW PERSPECTIVE

There isn't one simple sensation that comes from an experience. Each person brings with them their own touch and their own way of being. It is quite wonderful to understand that the body responds before the mind responds. In your gut, you feel the warmth, or the light, or whatever it is that you crave.

I used to think that you wouldn't want to spread yourself out all over the world in too many places. I have since changed my mind.

I now like to think that everybody has a different level of connection that they can offer and in intimacy we can decide how far in we will go with each person. During youth, it is hard to make the decisions about where you will end up going with things and how far in you will go.

That is the tough part. But there is beauty in giving yourself to someone in any way.

* * *

BECKONING PURPOSE

The beauty of this earth, as well as this life can be diminished when we start thinking that we need more than what is already present. Everything that you need in order to create yourself will come, whether it be through hard work or karmic ties. See, these memories we have serve as our books.

Love your book and write each page with intention. Do not allow the ink to become smeared with anything other than authenticity. Let go of the perception that you need grand objects or fame. Everything will unfold in a way that perfectly serves your souls' highest good. Regardless of the level of truth and transparency that you possess, how you decide to speak to and treat people, is what will ultimately build or destroy your stage.

* * *

INEVITABLE

I feel as though sometimes the best people do the worst things, like they have saved up all their bad for this horrible, inevitable worst.

* * *

UNRAVELLING

I think that in order to be who you are, you must know exactly what you are not. This, however, takes so much time and its slow process can deplete the ego.

When we find who we are, we sometimes have to apologize for the process that we took to understand ourselves. It can take years to do this.

We rewrite and erase what we think we know and who we are so often that we forget what the page originally looked like. I wonder sometimes, did I write with pen or pencil? I like to debate if my pages are marked with scribbled-over words or erase marks. I would assume it's a mixture of both, depending on which wolf I was feeding in myself.

* * *

HOW

There was a fragment of me, just a fragment that knew how it felt to be so broken and how I wanted to be fixed. I knew that sometimes it could even be by the person that hurt me in the first place, because it was still a try. It was a try at making peace with the past and what had mended my blood into calculated scars that spoke words by themselves. Even when something was already buried in stone, we had this idea that somewhere in the near future it could be brought back to life. Therefore, we could be brought back to life. However, before that, we knew we would have to release that pain and that seemed impossible.

* * *

WONDERING

It's because I wonder sometimes if you remember how I smelled or the way I moved. I wonder about whether or not you still want me, some part of me. I wonder when you started feeling like I meant something to you. I wonder if it was the real deal to you. I wonder if one day you will feel the pain that I felt and want me to come back, like I wanted you to come back. I wonder if you will understand why my head hurts at the thought of you. I wonder, if it will finally make sense to you why it didn't work out with us. I wonder, if you will make peace with your past, as I have my own. I wonder if your world will ever fit back into mine. I wonder if I will ever see myself the way I did before you. I wonder if you will be okay, because I am okay.

* * *

MESSY

I watched as he slipped right into oblivion. He couldn't grasp reality, and he couldn't enjoy it, especially not sober.

Originally, I thought it was about me and my own lacking. I slowly started to understand the abuse that had occurred between us. He didn't intend for any of it to occur but it was an unravelling mess.

In the midst of chaos, we were these two creatures of darkness sprinkled with light.

* * *

CORRELATION

I love you, and I will until the end of time.
You are stardust and madness.
I am pieces of glass and insanity.
We work, because we understand one another.
You see mine,
As clear as I see yours.

* * *

FEELING?

Bleeding out is nice, but it's slow and you can't always feel it. It's a process of awakening every wound and letting it all seep out.

There are pieces of glass that finally come out of you. There are pieces of wood or plastic that finally come out of you.

All of these little inconspicuous wounds start to become fresh again.

The feeling only lasts for a little bit though. Then you get the chance to patch yourself up.

The challenge is if you know how to stitch your body back together yourself.

* * *

FLORIST

Ours was not first or last, but rather the middle. We both wanted to keep what we had but we knew that we couldn't. For me, I hadn't seen enough yet. For you, you hadn't grown enough to know how to handle what we had.

I loved you and I still do love you. I think you are the first person who ever cracked me open and saw my guts. I had this feeling that I would pick someone who would hurt me and here we are.

One day, I will look back and understand. You didn't mean to hurt me and in my heart, I know that. But my ego and my fears tell me that I didn't mean what I thought I did. It's all illusion and I'm aware of that.

I saw you and I thought I was seeing my future and maybe I was. Now, I feel like my future is with me and ONLY me, at least for right now.

I'm blooming and I'm so fucking scared to wilt and dry up in the process. I promise I will find the water and the sun, and all things in between.

MINE, ETERNALLY

I'll always feel you around me. I think you made me this beautiful person because I was forced to feel better about myself.

I didn't like myself and then I changed everything because I knew that I had to decide to do that. I never wanted to be that person who feels that the screen is muted and there are tons of movies playing on every channel. The noise could be overbearing and unbearable, but I wanted to hear it.

People are used as catalysts for change in other people's lives and sometimes they get stuck in that role for way too long.

I feel like I almost got stuck in my own limbo of wanting more and asking for less. It's like a cycle of masochist awakening. I just wanted to hurt myself enough to feel. I wanted to feel rejected by people before I would even give them the chance to know how I felt or what I wanted.

NOT YET

If I could explain everything to him, I'd let him know how often I want to be held by him. I'd tell him that I wouldn't have become who I am today without him and that every piece of me loves him. I would also tell him to stop carrying the burden of everything, because it took both of us to cause the destruction that occurred.

I forgive him, for all of it. I wanted to be better, and I grew to be, but it was like catching someone in the middle of a job transition and expecting them to have tenure. I wasn't ready for him and I couldn't force myself to be.

* * *

UNBELIEVABLE

There's this fear.
I feel that no matter how hard I try,
I am not going to be good enough.
This is within me.
No matter the circumstance,
I find a way to see that I am inadequate.
You could write a book about me,
Complimenting my entire being,
And I would still deny that you meant it.

* * *

MYSTIC SELF

I tend to say that I don't settle, but I do. I settle for people and things that make me feel comfortable and secure. I am unsure of how to delve into certain waters. I know that if I do, I may not be able to swim on my own and it terrifies me and disturbs my ego. If I could force myself to do and be better, I would. However, I feel that I am sometimes in a rut of superficial self-examination. It's as if I have the idea and concept down, but I have no clue how to utilize it.

Within my own mind, I see all of this contradiction and it's bloodcurdling at times to acknowledge it. I worry that I will never merge the two opposing sides of myself and that I will become someone I do not like.

Maybe everybody fears this to some degree. We all have demons and we all face them at different times. The question I always have is this – Can you can decipher good from bad consistently throughout your life?

I feel that there are times that you simply cannot.

* * *

PLEASE

I hope to come back to you and to see things differently. You are the best love that I have ever experienced. Life is odd, because you don't know how to predict things and see when they will begin to change. You taught me that there is so much more to experience than physically being present. The love I have for you is something I will not be able to shake in one lifetime.

On this day, two years ago, I think I was still heartbroken over my first love. I was trying to examine how and when I would be able to move forward fearlessly.

Now, I am learning to let go of you. You were a much greater love to me than my first. You showed me the truth and the kindness in love. You are someone who I hope to find my way back to. You are the best person I have ever experienced.

Time changes so many things. I feel that I am finally learning myself in a way that I never have before. I am learning about how insecure I am, despite how strong I may feel at times. I used to think I was better than all of those little voices that would creep up in my head and I know that one day I will know this to be true again. In the meantime, I am learning to simply trust the process, as well as learning to trust myself.

ANSWERS

I want to know if letting go is something you get better with as you age. I want to know if time is an indicator of how much two people mean to one another. I want to know if there is a solid answer for certain questions. I want to know if there is a world in which everybody actually sees divinity in each other. I want to know the rhythm of independence and fate, as well as how to keep with it. I want to know who and what I am, in entirety.

I want to understand those who do the unimaginable. I want to understand the words of the past and speak with that kind of intention. I want to understand the mind that I was given. I want to understand how defeat is cultivated from creation.

* * *

IDENTITY

Hey there, do you see me?
I'm everywhere.
I'm you and them.
I am the ultimate end and the beast beginning.
I like to say I am love, or something like that,
But really, I am any real emotion that feeds the soul.
I am the thing every human craves,
And fears equally.

* * *

INDEPENDENCE

I think I understand why you did this, but it hurts too much to really look at it. You love me and you want to set me free. In idea, that is so amazing but it's hard to explain how bad it feels when it happens to you.

You can't just turn it off, all of the things you feel. I wish you could, but god only knows it isn't always that easy. When you grasp something so tightly, it becomes impossible to gather enough to let go. It's like you don't remember how your hand felt before you were holding that rope, or tie. I want so badly to hold on and I know can't. My hand is stretched so far out right now, clenching at air.

I don't know how to explain to you how things shatter people because it works differently for each person.

For me, it's like slicing emotions into thin pieces, so that I can take time processing each layer. There are so many layers that I hope I never get to, though.

PERPETUAL END

I wrote to you for years. I was hoping to find closure and hopefully some answers to cease all the questions in my head. It wasn't until I realized that it was fruitless to question someone who could not hear my voice, that I stopped trying.

It seems hard to analyze yourself when you have never seen things clearly. There is no script for becoming. I always assumed that I could stop myself from doing and being the wrong things, but it doesn't work that way. There is so much trial and error in that process.

There were a few years when I was desperately yearning to write myself into your life, so much so, that I forgot to write myself into my own. I wanted to be everything you wanted. This meant that I left no room to be what I wanted or dreamed of. It's the most pure form of self destruction, to not let yourself choose what you are.

When you let someone's perception of idealism skew how you want to be, you will always lose.

THE SELF LOVE

You won't be for everyone, but make sure you are for yourself. Cultivate an ocean of love for yourself to live in. There will be waves but if you can learn to swim in your own well, then the depth of others will not scare you.

Find something in yourself that makes you feel different. Find the dictionary definition of yourself, minus the B.S. Find something that gives you the letters in your name, or the inflection in your voice. It doesn't have to be something on you or about you, but it can be something you give to others. Maybe it is your ability to listen, or hug with such love, or perhaps giving others amazing advice. These are things that identify us and then connect us.

We, individually, make up this beautiful universe of souls.

In unison, we create this plethora of beauty, but alone we must first honor ourselves enough to shine without other stars.

SACRED

She said to me, "You are loved. You are loved. You are so, so, so, loved."

I said, "By who?"

She said, "By the earth, by the sky and by everything else."

I asked her why.

She said, "Because I am as well. I didn't know this until it was too late, so know this now. Please live in this knowledge, always."

* * *

THIS EXACT MOMENT

As I cried, he started holding my hand and tried to soothe me.

"We will be okay," he said.

"I don't want this to be the end," I cried.

"It isn't."

Through teary eyes, I asked him how he knew.

"It isn't raining, that means it isn't the end."

* * *

ANALOGY

It's like drowning. That's how I would explain heartbreak. You aren't dead but it feels as though you are grabbing for something out of reach. You want so badly to come up for air but you can't remember how to swim to the surface. So you blindly swim around trying to find your way up, only moving horizontally through the water. The water is so cold you think you might freeze, and you almost hope that you will so that you will tap out.

* * *

EGO MATCHES

I fight the jealousy in myself. I think it comes from my fear of being inadequate. I don't think we can gain much from comparison, but it is so easy to fall into it.

I want to support other women and I fight the want to be the best my partner has ever had. That is ignorant as hell, but it makes sense. If someone is wonderful, does that mean that they are better than me?

It's a constant "what if" in my mind. I debate my worth, along with every other person in the universe. At the end of the day, I find myself stuck in the idea that maybe all of us are equally as important. Maybe we each are different pieces of the world's puzzle, with different colors and markings. See, this way, we are all needed but we are all different. I just hope one day, I understand where my piece fits.

* * *

IF, ONLY

I kill time trying to analyze what I could or should have done. I keep assuming that I had the power to dictate certain situations.

However, in my heart of hearts, I know this to be untrue.

Controlling the way things occur is what I perceive as the best high. If you can control things, you can control whether or not you get hurt.

Nobody actually wants pain,

Even in a self-destructive pitfall.

However it happens,

It acts as collateral damage.

* * *

WHICH IS IT?

Wherever you are in your mind, please take me there.

I want to understand the process of your thoughts.

I want to hear how you form ideas in your head before you speak.

I want you to ruminate on the idea of me,
Before you say my name.

Take a few seconds, and hover on the thought of my body.

Take some time to illuminate all of my bones.

Do yourself a favor and light a path from my feet to my brows.

Dig yourself into my brain, and sit there for a few minutes.

Do you see me, or do you feel me?

REASONING

Why do we write about love? I believe it's because we all want it and somehow, we are still baffled by the concept of love. It's overwhelming to love so much so that it rips the carpet from underneath your feet. It's like waking up and remembering that you breathe the same air as this person. The person who you want so badly to become one with.

No matter how hard you try to define love, you can't find a completely solid definition, because it's almost elusive. Most feelings are elusive. You cannot truly explain love to someone who has never felt it.

I hope that love is something every person gets to experience, in their own way. Whether it be through family or through a relationship. I think it is the essence of so much more than we could ever imagine.

* * *

GROWTH

I tried for a long time to remove myself, from myself.
I wanted to become something entirely new.
In my mind,
I knew I couldn't do so. However,
I wanted to run from what I thought was killing me.
I wanted my thoughts to leave.
Then, I found this clue.
I realized how close I was to liberation,
As long as I could breathe clean air.
I had to allow myself to stop judging everything I was.
There could not be any progress if I kept thinking I was inadequate.
I had to be with what I was, and enjoy each piece of me.
As I worked harder to grow,
I realized the seeds were as wonderful as the grown plant.

* * *

EMOTIONAL PUBERTY

When you cry for so long about something or someone, you almost burn out. It's as if you couldn't possibly feel any more pain over this particular thing, but you can. It takes time to forget, and then all at once, you remember again.

Trauma takes unique forms and it has the ability to lie dormant for years. We find ways to cope and make amends with all of the parts of unanswered stories. It's not necessarily healthy, but we find a way to survive.

Then, in a weeping moment. It all comes back. Did you fall over? Are you bleeding out on the ground?

It's not a singular definition. The first time your pain is diminished, your light is so bright that you feel invincible for just a second. After that second though, it's as if something is missing from you for the rest of your life.

The initial heartbreaks of life are so powerful and so intense, that your body has muscle memory. It's the most insane sensation. You always know how it felt because you never really stopped feeling it, in short painful intervals.

Do we keep these little spurts of ache in our deepest memoirs of life?

I think so.

I'd like to see all people's. Then, I think I would actually understand why they do what they do. Until then though, it's all assumption. So we all assume things about everyone. The knowledge that we all live with our pain is uniting in some way though. It is a feeling of brotherhood and sisterhood to realize that the initiation into life is to feel torn apart by something.

* * *

BACK DOOR

Perhaps I merged with the characters that I saw. I wanted to be in a kind of madness and turmoil because it had been glamorized to my generation.

It took me years to understand how painfully disgusting insanity can be. I wanted it to be beautiful and wonderful because I could be like a story book character. I wanted to be like those girls who hid all of their hardship with makeup, sex or drugs. My problem was that I could not run from my problems and escape in that way. Instead of escapism, I was stuck in my mind and sat with myself and my thoughts all of the time.

There are plenty of times when I have wished to be someone who could sprint away. I would pray to become a robot who looks at others as pawns. I thought I would be a brilliantly sad story of a woman. I fight the urge to find the back door in every situation and to get as far out of town as possible.

However, I know I would never find my way back.

THROUGH ALL EYES

Did this day seem different ten minutes ago?

Does your perception change in the blink of an eye?

When I was young, my mother explained to me how important perception is and how it is skewed in a different way for everybody. She would use the analogy of how two people can see different things when they are looking outside of a window in a house, depending solely on what window they were looking out of. You see, they both would be telling the truth of what they saw, but the other would not be able to agree because they did not see the same thing. Regardless, both of them are right and each of them has their own truth.

In life, we want to think that some questions have solid answers and unfortunately they just don't. We have these firm ideas about what certain things should or could be, but that doesn't change what they are or what their potential could be. The lens through which people view their lives is thoroughly tainted by their own experiences and what they know.

I look at the world through the ideas that I got in my childhood, adolescence, and those that I continue to get. I cannot jump into someone else's mind and understand why or how they did what they did. There are times when I would like nothing more than to be another person for one specific day and understand the decisions they made or would make.

Eventually, I think, there are things that do make sense because time reveals how simple and mindless some decisions are. Or, we decide to be compassionate and live in the mindset of forgiveness.

As people, we ask to be forgiven about as much as we want to forgive others. This is one of the toughest lessons I have ever come across, and I am still learning it. Most religions preach compassion and kindness and that extends into forgiveness.

I pray to learn how to understand others and to heal myself through that.

* * *

MY TRUTH

To be honest, there hasn't been much that doesn't make me think of the person I used to be.

I'm reminded constantly of how open and beautiful my heart was before it was exposed. Perhaps now it is more of a broken picture frame up for sale.

I wanted to tell you everything, then and now. I wanted you to hear me cry and tell me that it meant something to you when I hurt.

I did all these things to make myself feel less alive and more numb to emotion. Now I see that the opposite is what would have saved me.

I should have been ready to see all of these phenomenal things this life has to offer.

Giving myself over to someone or something bigger than myself, has taught me that I cannot be ruined unless I allow myself to be.

I believe in a love that mends and creates new beginnings as well as brings back old feelings of security.

Yes, I believe that love is painful and that we must fight for a long time, in order to understand that. But I also believe that is what makes us grateful for the big great love that we may experience one day.

And if not, I sure do hope I catch enough love from those around me to ensure that I understand the point of it all.

Unconditional love, in any form, is a stimulant.

* * *

FUTURE-TENSE

Today, I am going to wake up and see his face. Tomorrow, I am going to wake up and see his face.

Next month or maybe next year, I am going to wake up and I will see my face. I will put my makeup on and I will walk away from my house feeling better about myself and the world. I will be a better woman and better person.

I am still waiting for that day. In the meantime though, I am learning a lot about memories and how the mind works to protect us from pain. I notice how I can almost completely forget certain people who have hurt me and others I cannot even begin to forget. A therapist once told me that our mind will find ways to protect us and keep us safe and there are several ways of doing so.

In this moment, I am trying to find my mechanism to forget you.

* * *

INSIDE

It's strange, because I am 19. However, I feel so old and almost jealous of who I used to be. I want to be that person again. I'm not sure if I am attracted to the unscathed blueprint or the unshattered heart, but I yearn to be younger again. That's insane right? I am so young.

It's terrifying to have everything at your fingertips because you always want what is coming next, and you don't enjoy moments. I think about how I am constantly wanting to graduate college and how I am anticipating that day. Then, it dawns on me and scares the living shit out of me that I will probably be anticipating another event almost as soon as I accomplish that. It's like we live to become something else, all of the time. I guess that is the point. The strange part, is that we aren't built to use ourselves in order to use others, or pawn ourselves for money. Yet, that is all we do. We don't have community or a sense of friendship in the way that, I assume, we did a long time ago. I strive for that, constantly.

Sometime in the future, I'll have a baby of my own and I'll have to explain the process of all of this to them. The good thing is that I won't have to explain it all at once. I will have so much time to piece the world together for them and maybe map it out. I want to think that is what parents are supposed to, that is their job. They try to paint the picture to their children of what the world really is, even though it is ever changing. And despite how messy it may be while adding in new color, there is always a beautiful blending occurring. I want to say that the horizons we meet on as people are equivalent and comparable, but I doubt it. We are all unique, and we see the world as we see it. I hope to one day see it in an even better way than I do now, and to send that to my children and so on. The cycle itself, of all of this, is never ending but also so strongly and clearly a death in itself. There is no escaping that. So we live, as much as we can, and feel as much as we can. So that the little things in the middle, like waiting to graduate college, are not necessarily milestones but moments that give us great feelings of being present.

I want so badly to be present in this life, and I feel myself getting closer, every day.

* * *

FULL CIRC-

When I was crying, I felt myself shatter into so many little pieces. I physically did not know how I would ever be whole again. There isn't something that could have fixed me, in any way.

See, broken people are often the ones that seek other broken people and feel connected to them before they do anybody else. Broken attracts broken. It's a circle of people meeting each other and creating more and more of a story.

I wait for the day that I find someone who will draw something other than a circle with me. I want it to be a line. I want us to be two lines, parallel to one another, and never ending.

* * *

KNOWLEDGE, THEN POWER

Tell me how to do it.
Tell me how I can calm the sound of my mind.
Tell me how I can become the person I want to be.
Tell me that it gets better, at least at some point.
Tell me the way you did it, and how you came through it all.
Tell me the words I can say to myself, to fix these broken thoughts.
Tell me the least frightening though you have had.
Tell me that you understand how hard it can be to stop yourself.

* * *

EMPATHY

This is so melodramatic. Then again, this is also how I feel. It's hard to take away emotions and feelings, especially once you have thoroughly identified them. However, I pray to feel things in a way that won't debilitate me. Within the same breath, I am grateful though. The ability that I have to feel is part of what defines me as a person. It is like one of my limbs.

* * *

MY SWEET LOVE

There was a moment when I knew that I would always love you. I don't fully remember what happened, but the sensation remains the same.

You had hands that could hold every part of me. I wanted to melt like sand into your ocean.

You were so kind and so beautiful. I had every desire to lay my soul to rest with yours when the time came.

You were all of the things that I knew, as well as all of the things that I wanted to know. For that, I know that my soul will always remember yours.

* * *

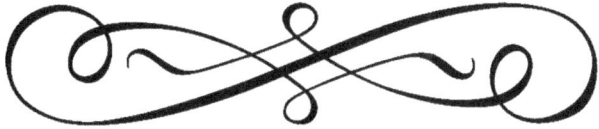

www.ingramcontent.com/pod-product-compliance
Lightning Source LLC
Chambersburg PA
CBHW061249040426
42444CB00010B/2322